Let's go to the fair!

Finger-trace along the path to help the Letterlanders get to the fair.

Finger-tracing — Encourage your child to trace the route with his or her finger to get used to going from left to right and top to bottom. Talk about the scene. There's Harry Hat Man hurrying to the fair. Find Clever Cat in her car and Annie Apple in her apple tree.

Fairground food

Trace along the paths in the Reading Direction.

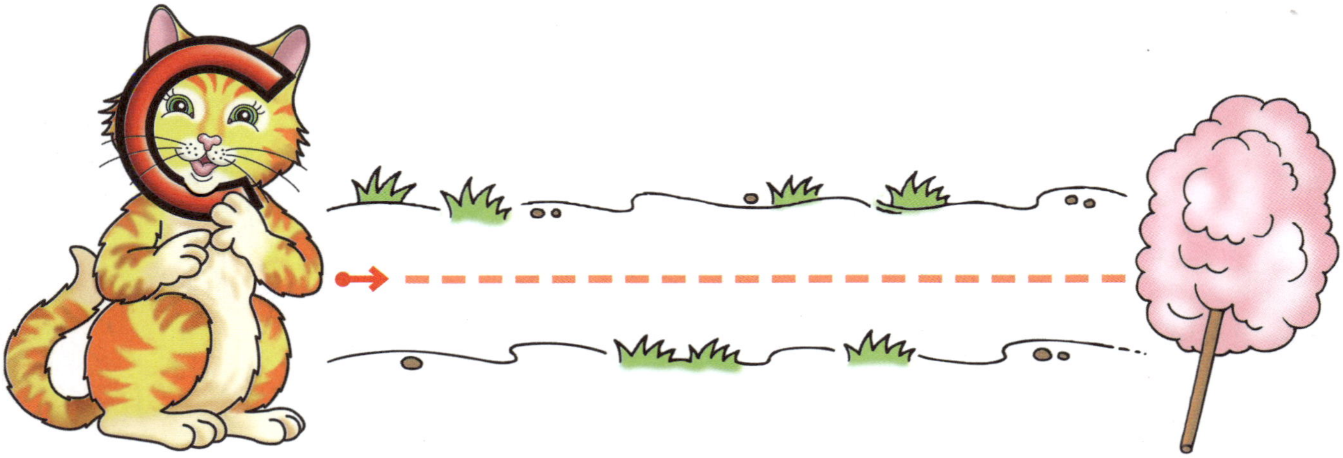

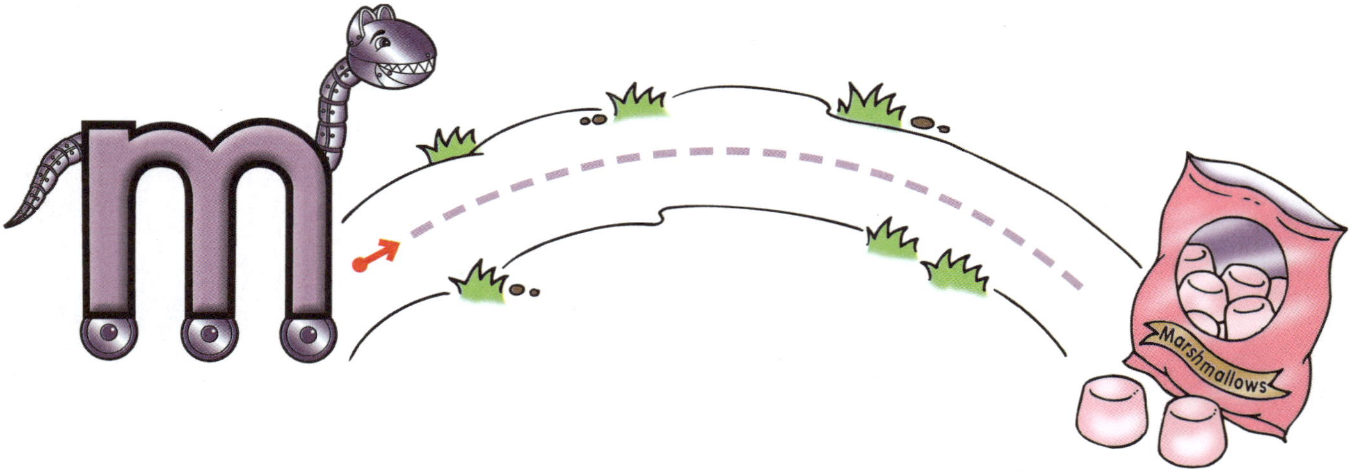

First sounds

The Letterlanders love to eat things that start with their sounds. Emphasise the sounds as your child traces each path from left to right, e.g. **C**lever **C**at loves **c**andyfloss. **D**ippy **D**uck loves **d**elicious **d**oughnuts. What might **M**unching **M**ike like?

Letterland races

Reading Direction →

Trace along the paths in the Reading Direction.

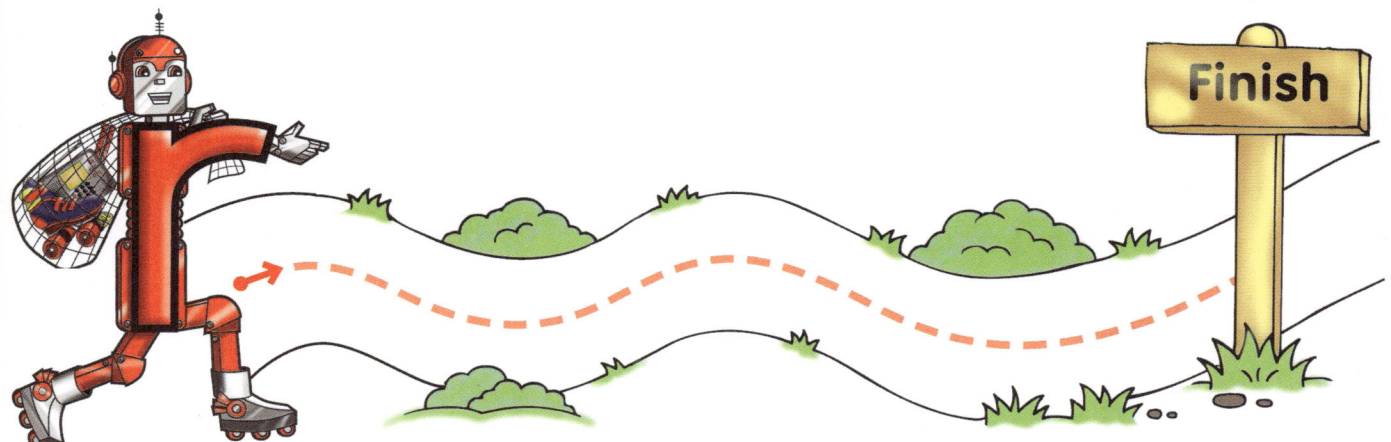

More sounds — Talk about each character as your child traces each path. **R**ed **R**obot is **rrr**acing to the finish! Will **T**alking **T**ess be **t**alking all the **t**ime as she runs? Why is **W**alter **W**alrus **w**addling down, up, down, up? Encourage your child to make one continuous line.

3

Sammy's slippery slides

Trace down the slides.

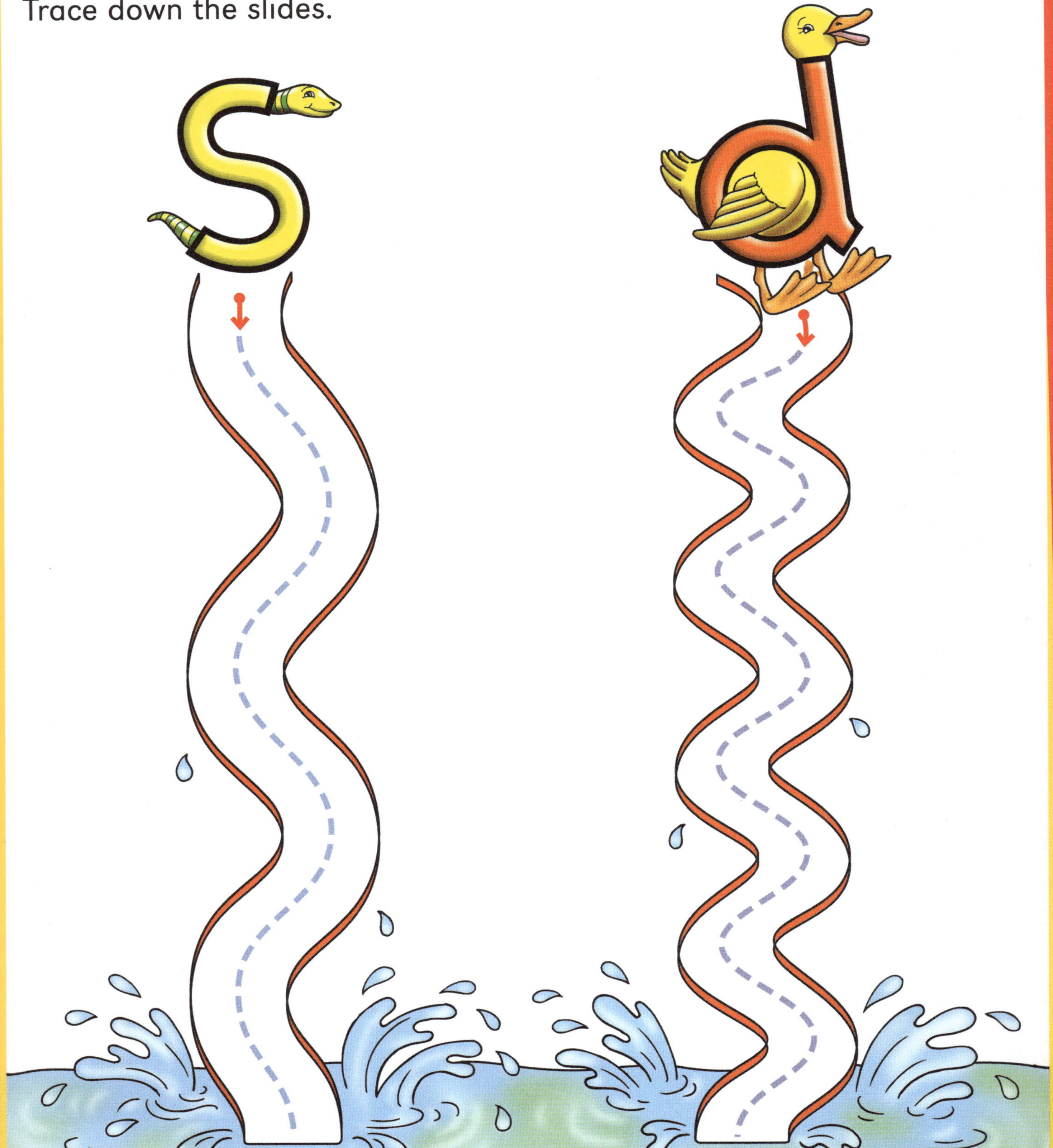

Sammy Snake and Dippy Duck love the water. **D**ippy loves to **d**ive **d**own **d**eep in her **d**uckpond and **S**ammy loves **sss**wimming in the **s**ea! Encourage your child to say 'sss...' and 'd..., d...' as he or she traces the lines from top to bottom.

Harry's helicopter hats

Trace over the lines.

Harry's shape & sound

Tracing straight lines will help when your child comes to writing letters that start with a straight line, e.g. l and h. Harry Hat Man has a hat shop where he makes all kinds of hats. He has even made a huge hat into a roof for his house (see page 1)!

Ben's bouncy castle

Trace over the lines.

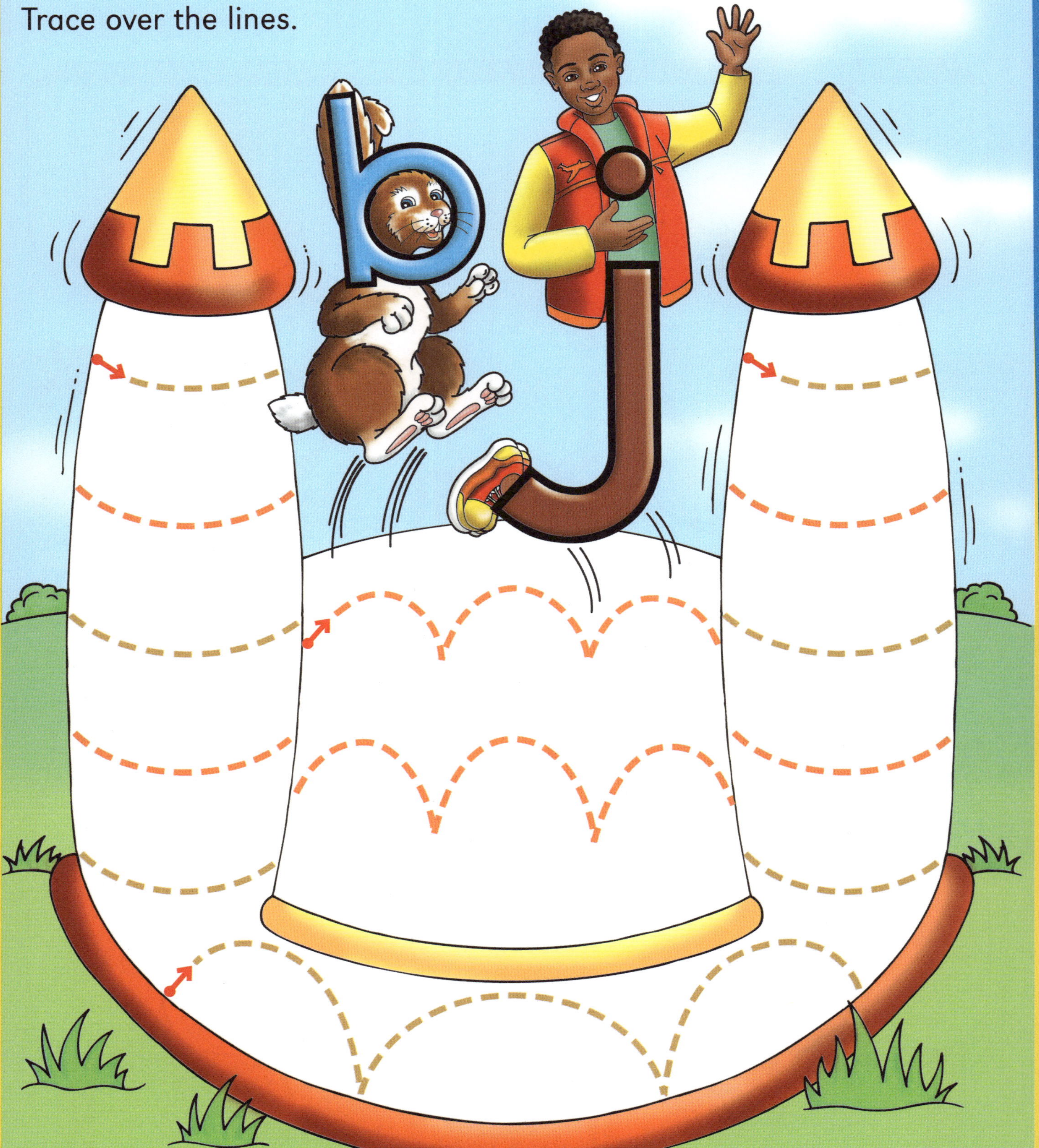

This activity introduces the slightly more difficult 'bouncy' pattern. **B**ouncy **B**en loves **b**ouncing **b**est. **B**oing! **B**oing! **B**oing! **J**umping **J**im loves to **j**ump. He can **j**ump as high as a **j**et!

Lucy's lollipops

Trace over the lines.

Tracing these patterns helps to develop pencil control. Encourage your child to say Lucy Lamp Light's 'lll...' sound as he or she traces the l-shape from top to bottom. Ask: Which of these lovely lollipops would you like to lick?

Lucy's sound & shape

Fred's fishing game

Trace over the lines.

Continuous lines

Encourage your child to trace these patterns in one continuous line. In his free time, Firefighter Fred's favourite thing to do is fishing. Noisy Nick and Oscar Orange think it's fun to fish, too!

Eddy's egg game

Reading Direction

Trace along the lines.

Eddy's sound & shape

Eddy Elephant loves to play this egg-throwing game. Can your child remember the names of the other two Letterlanders? (Look at the inside back cover, if help is needed.) This pattern may need extra practice as the pencil direction changes.

Letterland castle

Trace over the lines.

Kicking King and Quarrelsome Queen are the king and queen of Letterland. They live in a big castle with Kicking King's pet kangaroo. Can your child spot Vicky Violet and Walter Walrus? Can he or she say each letter's sound?

Max's box game

Trace over the lines. Who does each box belong to?

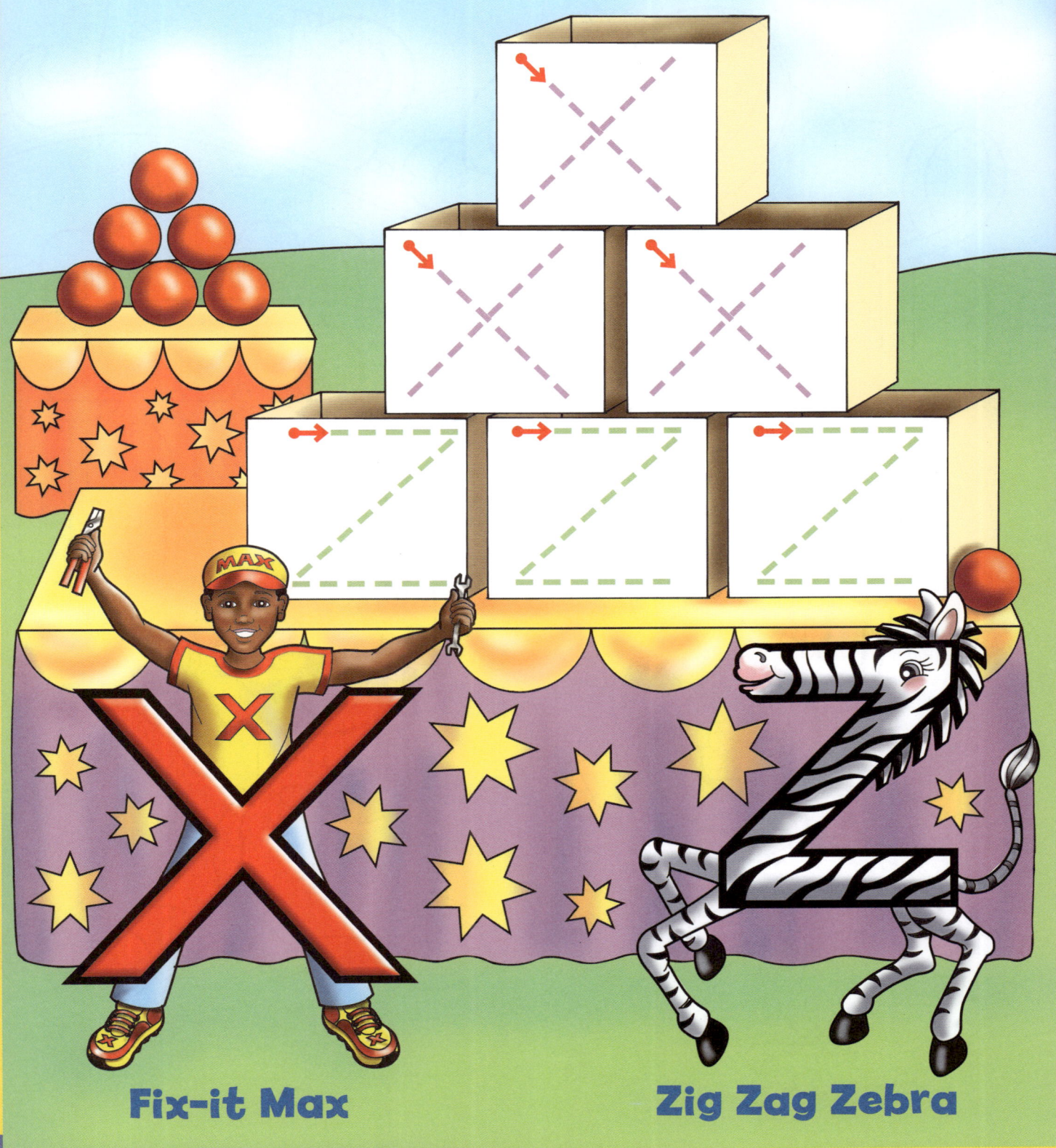

Fix-it Max

Zig Zag Zebra

Straight line letters — Max's letter and Zig Zag Zebra's letter are both made of straight lines. Can your child write more of their letter shapes on a piece of paper? Can he or she make some patterns using these two letters?

At the fair

Colour the picture.

Pencil control — Colouring helps to practise pencil control. Which Letterlanders can your child spot? Finger-trace their letters and say their sounds.

Harry's helter skelter

Trace over the lines.

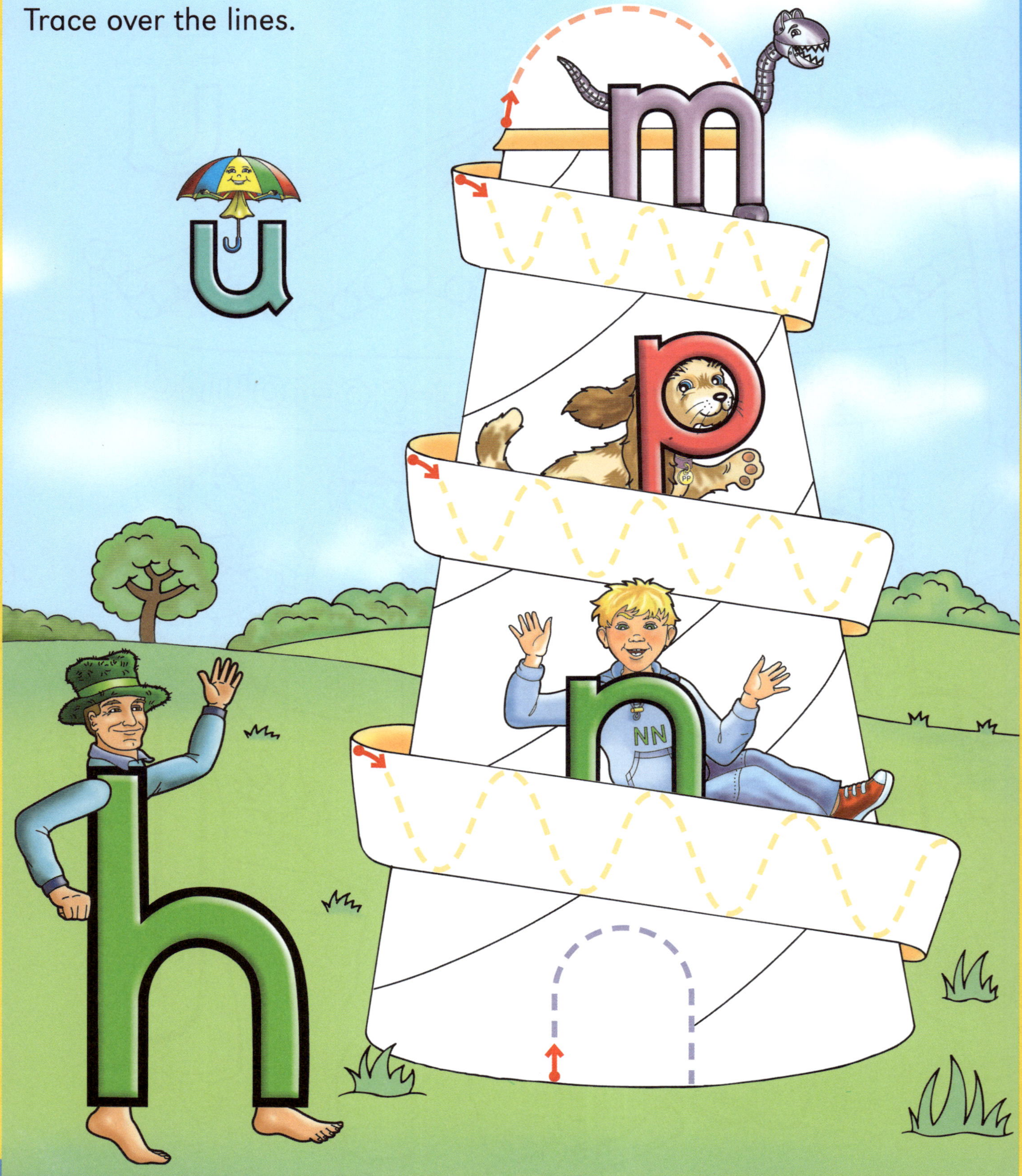

Can your child remember the names of the Letterlanders coming down the helter skelter? Who is that up in the air? (Look at the inside back cover if you need help.) Practice using these patterns will help when your child comes to write the letters.

Mike's merry-go-round

Trace over the lines.

Look — Who is on **M**unching **M**ike's **m**erry-go-round? Encourage your child to finger-trace Red Robot and Bouncy Ben's letters before starting the handwriting patterns.

Pattern play

Trace over the lines.

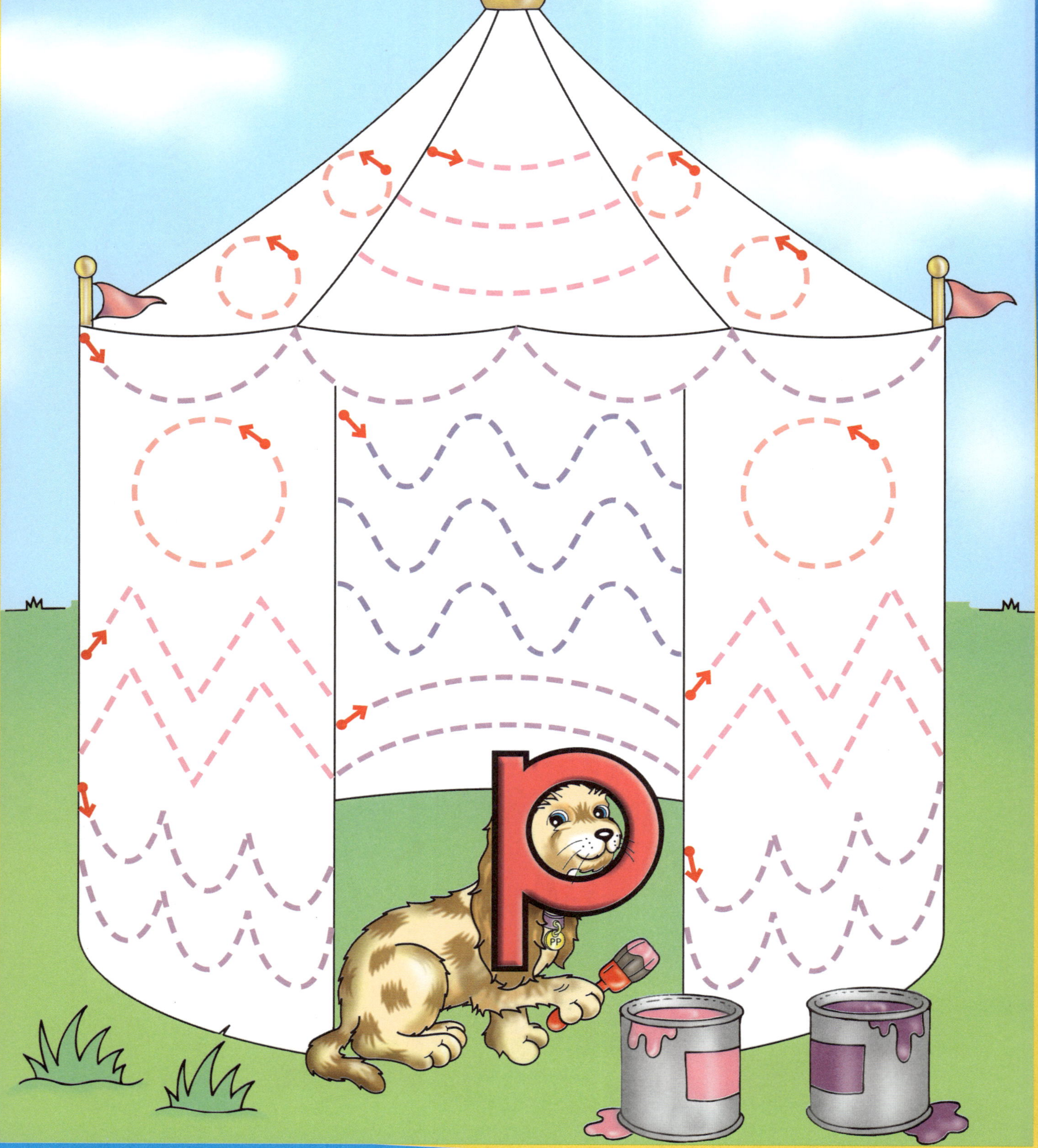

Peter **P**uppy is **p**ainting **p**atterns. What colours do you think he likes best? (**P**ink and **p**urple of course!) Encourage your child to try writing these handwriting patterns on a plain piece of paper as well.

Look and find

Tick the box when you find:

a monkey ☐ a lollipop ☐

some flowers ☐ an egg ☐ a fish ☐

Who is quarrelling with a squirrel?   Who is holding balloons?

Letter sounds

Letterlanders love things that start with the first sound in their name, e.g. **Mmm**unching **Mmm**ike ... **mmm** ... **mmm**onkey. See if your child can guess which Letterlanders would like objects you see around you in your home.

The l letter family

All our letters start the same way.

Reading Direction →

down

down

down

Before writing the letter, encourage your child to finger-trace over each one, starting at the top of the arrow. Remind your child to lift the pencil off before crossing the **t** (in the Reading Direction) and to go back and dot the **i** and **j**.

The letter family

"All our letters start the same way."

Reading Direction →

 around

 around

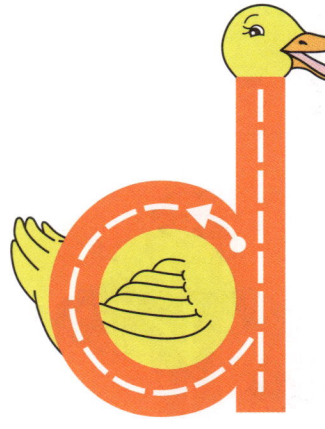 around

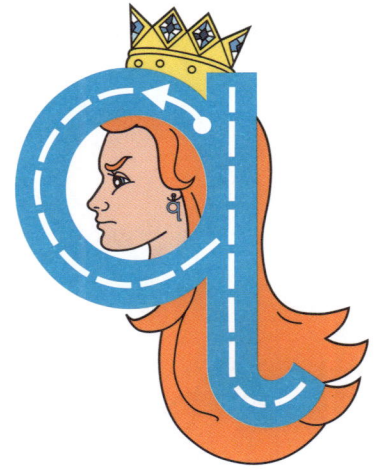

Writing letters — Finger-tracing in the correct sequence helps to develop good handwriting habits right from the beginning. Remind your child to lift the pencil off before crossing the **f** with a stroke in the Reading Direction.

21

The  letter family

"All our letters start the same way."

 down

 up

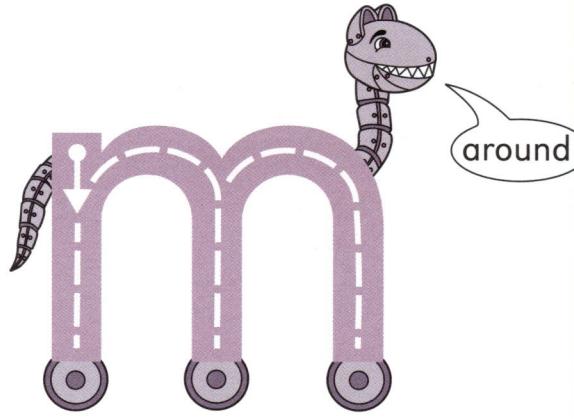 around

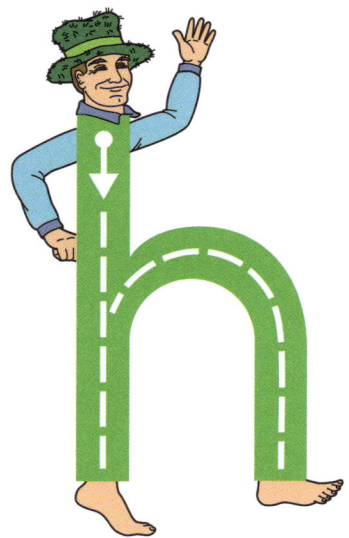

Encourage your child to finger-trace each letter first. A good time to practise a letter's sound is while finger-tracing it.

The zigzag family

"All our letters are straight lines."

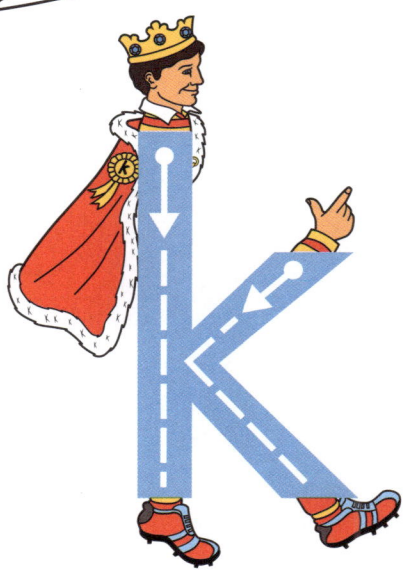

Writing letters

After finger-tracing and writing over all the letter families, encourage your child to go over these pages again, saying the sounds together with you as he or she writes over the letters again.